Summary of

12 Rules for Life: An

Antidote to Chaos By

Jordan B. Peterson

SpeedyReads

Note to readers:

This is a SpeedyReads guide to Jordan Peterson's "12 Rules for Life: An Antidote to Chaos" meant to enhance your reading experience. You are encouraged to buy the original book.

Claim Your Free Gift Now

As a way of saying "thank you" for your purchase, we're offering you a free special report that's *exclusive* for our book readers.

In **"Delicious Reading: How to Quadruple and Enhance Your Book Reading Experience Within 24 Hours"**, you'll discover simple but powerful ways to heighten and enhance your book reading experience that was only known by the top book connoisseurs…. Until now…

Go to the link below before it expires!

http://www.easysummaries.com/gift

Summary of 12 Rules for Life: An Antidote to Chaos

Contents

Claim Your Free Gift Now

Summary of 12 Rules for Life

12 Rules for Life: Rule 1 - Stand up Straight with Your Shoulders Back

12 Rules for Life: Rule 2- Treat Yourself Like Someone You Are Responsible for Helping

12 Rules for Life: Rule 3- Make Friends with People Who Want the Best for You

12 Rules for Life: Rule 4- Compare Yourself to Who You Were Yesterday, Not To Who Someone Else Is Today

12 Rules for Life: Rule 5- Do Not Let Your Children Do Anything That Makes You Dislike Them

12 Rules for Life: Rule 6- Set Your House in Perfect Order Before You Criticize the World

12 Rules for Life: Rule 7- Pursue what is Meaningful (Not what is Expedient)

12 Rules for Life: Rule 8- Tell the Truth- or At Least, Don't Lie

12 Rules for Life: Rule 9- Assume That The Person You Are Listening To Might Know Something You Don't

12 Rules for Life: Rule 10- Be Precise in Your Speech

12 Rules for Life: Rule 11- Do Not Bother Children When They Are Skateboarding

12 Rules for Life: Rule 12- Pet a Cat When You Encounter One on the Street

Background Information about the Summary of 12 Rules for Life: An Antidote to Chaos

Background Information about the Author: Jordan B. Peterson

Discussion Questions about the Summary of 12 Rules for Life: An Antidote to Chaos

Do you want special deals?

FINAL SURPRISE BONUS

Summary of 12 Rules for Life

Human being does not like rules in general despite knowing that they benefit us. We do not want a lot of rules. However, without rules, we are likely to lose a sense of direction and go wayward. Therefore, we need rules.

12 Rules for Life: Rule 1 - Stand up Straight with Your Shoulders Back

The example of lobsters indicate that they reside on the floor of the ocean since they need something secure to serve as a hub where they can hunt. However, since a huge number of lobsters exist, a complication arises if two or more lobsters occupy the same territory. If hundreds of lobsters attempt to hunt for food and keep a family in the same place, it will lead to chaos. Such territorial disputes also apply to the example of songbirds.

The example of chickens also indicates that identities play a critical role in the survival of birds as well. Those who preferred availability of food in the morning are the most important chickens owing to their visible superiority. The second most important are those that come a close second. The hierarchy goes down and the last are the chickens that are in a bad condition, they have a small amount of feathers left, etc. A dominance hierarchy is evident. Songbirds do not live collectively like chickens but the healthiest and most powerful of them have control over the main territory and shield it.

Over the course of millennia, animals that face a requirement to exercise cohabitation with others within the perimeters of a territory have learned several tricks to settle dominance with the least quantity of loss, handling conflict in their own ways.

The neurochemistry of a lobster that wins is different from that of a lobster that loses and the levels of serotonin and octopamine makes a difference in this context. The principle of unequal distribution accentuates when a lobster that lost earlier recollects its courage and battles again, the probability of it losing again is high. A winning lobster will most probably win again. The same principles apply to the human financial world, where the few richest people on the planet have the same wealth as the billions of people that are at the bottom. The same pattern is evident in other fields such as science, music, etc., where a small number of people dominate a field in the form of its mastery. This principle is also known as Price's law.

Furthermore, female lobsters recognize the most significant male rapidly and are irrevocably attracted to him. Females of other species including humans also do this. They leave it to the dominance hierarchy to figure out who the best man is and let the males battle it out. This applies to the stock market as well. When the females are prepared to mate, they try to attract the dominant lobster with different tactics. The successful one gets the male. Since lobsters have been around for several million years, it shows that dominance hierarchies have existed since time immemorial and all complex forms of life had to adjust to it. This highlights that even though brains and nervous systems were quite simple earlier, they still had the neurochemistry and structure required to take details pertaining to status and society into account.

Confidence plays an extremely significant role in helping the fittest survive. Those with the right mindset and internal features succeed. Those who feel that they are not up to the mark are likely to fail. The occurrences in an individual's life get registered in their brain as good or bad. If an individual expects people to be nice since they are nice themselves, they are wrong and likely to face a fall since it does not work that way. People need to reinforce themselves and stand up so that they will not get caught up in a circle of failures.

12 Rules for Life: Rule 2- Treat Yourself Like Someone You Are Responsible for Helping

Humans are usually more concerned about the health of their loved ones than themselves. They would readily assist a loved one but will not give themselves the same treatment. It poses an issue. Further, it is just recent that human being started giving more importance to scientific information than history. Prior to that, historical texts made humans feel for centuries. Humans and the things around them tend to be subjective. Human consciousness, a sense of chaos and order govern the universe at the same time. Order is linked with things happening in an identical manner, and chaos is anything that disrupts order and harmony. Nevertheless, chaos spawns a different kind of order even though it does not appear to do that on the surface.

Order shares its qualities with the male owing to the certainty of the configuration while chaos shares its qualities with the female owing to the fact that it can spawn new universes, which can be good or bad. Finding a sense of 100% stability between order and chaos leads to success and a disproportion between two can lead to issues.

An example of Eve and the fact that she led to Adam to a fall and her own exit from paradise indicates that women make men accomplish what they are meant to and give rise to lessons. The existence of a snake is worth noting in this context. Also, Adam was aware of his identity and today's human beings are too. Humans are further aware of the definition of good and evil since God gave them an ability to differentiate between the two. This form of consciousness enables humans to be aware of what is good for themselves and others. This spawns the dilemma as to why they ignore their own selves. Humans believe that others deserve their love and praise since it is ingrained in their configuration. They do not realize that they hold an equal amount of significance. They need to realize that they have the divine inside themselves too like others and refrain from harming themselves unknowingly.

12 Rules for Life: Rule 3- Make Friends with People Who Want the Best for You

The example of Fairview, Alberta shed light on the detail that before various channels of entertainment exist in today's time, people interacted with one another a lot. During winters, people got sad and frustrated and people and animals died a lot, deaths stemming from drinking in the former. The author shared the example of his friend Chris and his cousin Ed, who were gifted but did not realize their potential owing to the use of Marijuana, etc. The town did not offer the youth prospects and most people just had a wish to bid adieu to the town. Nothing including attachment and the chance to interact so much with others could boost the morale of those living there.

Chris's life went downhill from there and despite being extremely intelligent; he brought an end to his life. This might have resulted from the fact that people around him transformed and he did not believe that things would improve. On the contrary, the writer of the book realized the importance of friends that matter and want to travel on an upward slope. Having this kind of friends made the writer give increased importance to studies and their translation into something more substantial. This gave birth to a circle of improvement for him.

If people do not want to improve their conditions themselves, others cannot do it for them. They make a statement to others that they do not want things to improve in the form of their friends. Those who are destined to fail encounter people that are failures themselves and do not want to help anyone to be better or better themselves with the assistance of anybody else. Therefore, friendship is the kind of thing where both parties wish to act in the best interests of the other. If any of the parties does not wish to be witness to other's success, there is an issue. One needs to discover the kind of friends that would help them reach new heights instead of making them go down.

12 Rules for Life: Rule 4- Compare Yourself to Who You Were Yesterday, Not To Who Someone Else Is Today

An individual might feel demotivated since another individual is better at something that the first person has been doing for a long time. But it may cause the first person to experience chaos. This is not the proper way. Furthermore, it is not necessary for a person to excel at all the things. An individual may have a lot to handle, more than they can take. A human being may excel at one thing and face unfavorable circumstances as far as something else is concerned. This can lead to envy for others as well for being better at something. People need to realize that they need to learn to accept if others are successful at something since they also have successes to celebrate at something else.

What individual needs to realize here is to let go of the past since the person cannot do anything to change it. There is also a need to view the future as something with an infinite sense of promise. In addition, a person also needs to be aware of their positive and negative aspects. They need to focus on improving the negative to accomplish something. They also need to take one thing at a time and celebrate small wins.

While observing something, we see what we wish

to and ignore the rest. We have a huge scope and range where we can succeed but we limit ourselves by focusing on one thing. When we fail at that thing, it makes us frustrated. We need to consider that life goes beyond that. People face a requirement to find a balance between the positive and the negative. In other words, they must surpass their gloomy and negative approach to accomplish something in life. People need to have a bigger scope and range since a huge number of phenomena govern their lives. Since a person can select something from a huge number of things that results into failure, this can further cause frustration. The other option is nice and easy i.e. selecting something else that would make their life less chaotic and make things better. It will also lead to joy and provide them with a direction until they reach their real target. Joy holds more weight and substance

than a mere win.

12 Rules for Life: Rule 5- Do Not Let Your Children Do Anything That Makes You Dislike Them

As a parent, you have full authority over how your children turn out to be. The early part of a child's life is extremely important in this context. If you do not control your child in the start, such a kind of child will not be able to derive order from chaos later and if you discipline your child initially, it will enable him or her to easily derive order from chaos.

Even though everyone wants a well-mannered child, it is not an easy task. Despite parents trying so hard to control children, children end up being undisciplined. This gives rise to a need for letting go of old rules to pave the way for a new approach.

The example of animals indicates that when left desolate, they can invoke conflict and form hierarchies. This should not be so in human beings. Homo sapiens need to direct their children with the assistance of their care and attention. This can help children battle instincts and the negative effects of their surroundings. A parent is accountable for shaping their child's manners and outlook. Parents in today's times believe that they need to give their children complete independence but this is not how it should be. This can lead to negative behavior patterns in a child. Shaping the right kind of child is much more challenging than the wrong one since bad behaviors are easier. It remains the duty of a parent to shape a child to be good since they are the only one that can do it. In today's times, a lot of parents are not aware of the harm they can cause their child by their inability to drive their child to be good. By punishing and rewarding children, parents can teach them what is right and wrong. This leads to a broader lesson for life in terms of what is right and wrong in the eyes of people. This can shape all interpersonal and personal aspects of life. In the course of existence, children need stern direction from someone at times. This gives rise to the need for forceful action on the part of the parents if the child is not acting in accord with the norms of society. This force aiming to discipline, if properly regulated, will not cause the child to be aggressively inclined.

Parents do not need a huge list of rules. A small number of rules will suffice. In addition, rather than being a single parent, parents need to be accompanied by another parent to complete the equation. Parents can leave a sad effect on their children if their circumstances are gloomy. They are further accountable for the social abilities of their children.

Parents need to tolerate their children since no one else would. They need to make their children socially balanced, which will also assist the child in being balanced overall.

12 Rules for Life: Rule 6- Set Your House in Perfect Order Before You Criticize the World

Existence is full of suffering and this is seen in the form of the numerous shootings that have been witnessed at multiple places in the USA alone. While people claim a religious allegation to such incidents, the reason is never good enough to mock the Creator in such a manner. The suffering of others and self might be assumed often as consequential but that is not always the truth, so the suffering becomes unfair and so does the intent for such actions.

What happens to a person once they have

undergone some form of suffering is totally up to them because it is their mind that will make up the decisive vote in the end. History is full of people who took a turn for the worst as they went after all those who took advantage of them in any manner; these people initiated a negative cycle of actions that lead to further evils. On the other hand, there were many (like Aleksandr Solzhenitsyn) who spread kindness in exchange with torture, to eliminate the very existence of torture.

A fully functional society and individual would keep himself in check over his actions and ensure that the actions are in no way negligent towards what is required from him. Negligence to duty would ultimately lead to a state where the individual would ultimately fall into a condition of suffering. However, if one desires to blame fate then one can do so but it needs to be remembered that actions lead to reactions.

The charm of life for most is in pointing out just what others are doing wrong. Stop this action immediately if you desire to shake out of the stupor of momentum lacking life. The best way to proceed in real life is to assess personal actions and see if they are good or evil in their context. Stop the evil acts since the human heart guides how right or wrong a thing is inherently. Limiting and then ending such acts of deterioration would ultimately lead to a state where daily life would become productive and it will also serve as a source of happiness in the personal, social and business facets of life.

12 Rules for Life: Rule 7- Pursue what is Meaningful (Not what is Expedient)

If humans were to look back to their origins, they would see that they had been cursed long before coming to earth and so, their life would end and not remain and so would none of their deeds. So, why not live to your fullest potential?

Save for the future. Yes, it would satisfy the animalistic tendencies in human beings if they were to get whatever they wanted, within a wink of time. But is it really good? What if money saved today and helps out in getting food tomorrow? The values one has dedicated to one's priorities. If a person is unhappy all the time, they should think about changing what they value.

Human suffering is vast and wholesome. The cycle started with the origins of humans. Humans did not know that they were bad but then they had to face depreciation for the lack of effort they put in their work. Humans then forwarded the wound to other humans and so, suffering became a part of humans.

The success of humans lies in not giving in to the whispers of 'Satan' or rather in refraining from taking shortcuts as they limit the future outlook of their actions. Christianity provided its followers with the best routes to adhere to for solving their problems but through these passages, humans found themselves standing at a new valley where the rules have to change for the sake of survival. At this point, a human owns his functions because Christ's guidance cannot help him.

Religion, while bringing to light all that is evil, left the humans wondering what is good. The religions of the past do not help the humans get out of their present suffering. To get out of the sufferings, it falls upon the humans to sacrifice and do anything to prevent evil from occurring.

Humans sin all the time. Once humans start doing things after they understand the meanings of their actions, they have a different view of their actions and their impacts in the future; this tends to stimulate them to continuously do good all the time.

12 Rules for Life: Rule 8- Tell the Truth- or At Least, Don't Lie

Often, it is the truth that saves one's skin and it is in one of these times that the human mind latches on to the importance of saying the truth. Lies always end up hurting someone as in the case of the author's paranoid client. Truth frees the human mind as they do not have to think twice or worry about hiding something actively. A lie that a person likes apple pie would result in the hostess offering the most amount of that pie to the person, resulting in a defeat for the person.

The author lived in a rented space along with his wife. The owner of this space lived next door and was an alcoholic trying to stop his drinking habit. The neighbor was also an ex-convict. The neighbor would visit the author at 3 or 4 in the morning whenever he ran out of money and would sell the author things so that he would have the money to buy more booze. The author continued to buy things until one day he declined for the sake of his wife. He told his neighbor the truth about why he was stopping the money. The truth strengthened their relation later.

Living a lie does not help anyone at all. If one continues to believe in a lie and base one's life on that very lie, one will just ends up increasing the suffering that would happen as a result of the said lie. Making up reasons where there are none or making up stories to humor a crowd about self's wonderfulness; everything can come back to the person in one manner or another and ask for its due.

Human should learn to be true to themselves if they want to get themselves ahead in this world or in the next. Lying to self is dangerous and harmful for the person as it would lead to hell, but what does it do in this world? It takes away life bit by bit until a time comes when the individual cannot come to recognize the truth himself, leading to the ultimate decline. Even if one cannot state the truth, one should state anything else but a lie.

12 Rules for Life: Rule 9- Assume That The Person You Are Listening To Might Know Something You Don't

Advice is something that no one wants. The advisor is incidentally someone who places themselves on a pedestal that allows them to have an intellect above the one being advised. On the other hand, psychotherapy is counted as productive even when advice from it might not be as directed as advice.

Thinking alone is hard according to the author. The best way to go about thinking is when someone comments on how right or wrong a particular thought is. This type of vocal thinking allows best ideas to propagate and the duller ones to settle down. While a therapist is the best person to talk to and discuss one's thoughts with, they have been told by Freud not to be the one to inflict personal biases upon the patient that comes to them with his/her troubles. The advisor has to be objective of what is being said, focus on telling what looks like the truth objectively and try not to deviate the patient towards what he/she thinks is the truth of the situation.

Listening is a discipline in itself because it requires an unbiased presence from the listener. Carl Rogers realized that minimizing the truth spoken by the patient and presenting to him the more refined and connected version of the truth spoken by the patient actually helps everyone.

Listening is an element that is not always apparent in every conversation since most conversations are just a series of reactions to the original prompt of the conversation. The reactions in turn are aligned in such a manner that the new speaker tries to one up the previous speaker. Basically, this type of conversation is a battle of wits.

Another type of conversation, a favored one at that, involves two parties that desire to evolve the chaos of the world into an ordered condition. There is a dialogue in these conversations where both the parties provide the truths of life that they have learned so far. Both parties respect and take something from the conversation.

12 Rules for Life: Rule 10- Be Precise in Your Speech

Everything is evolving. What is relevant at the moment would not be relevant about half a century from now. Yet it should not be forgotten that the current institutions, physical or otherwise, are a result of the current environment; the environment comes together and helps run things the way they do.

Perceptions of a human being matter in every case, whether living or nonliving. What people perceive to be a part of them, matters to them at a personal level. Social connections with a group further dictate the actions and the perceptions of the individual as he/she becomes a part of the whole.

Humans do not understand the vastness of what they have until it starts malfunctioning in some manner. It is the distress that shows humans the complexities of a given thing not known and is yet to learn. The picture of normalcy can collapse within a minute and that is exactly how the human comes in contact with the reality of the universe. The universe is complex and once the human is exposed to the cruelties, they have to learn to cope.

There are many things that contribute to the ultimate collapse of a person's relations; one cannot simply continue to blame multiple things as that tends to further confuse them. The possibilities of what could have saved the relation would drown the human in misery if that happens.

Acceptance of present condition matters because only then can a person go about and learn to heal. The misconceptions that people hold dear to them are often the cause of their troubles.

The troubles should be pointed out for what they are, and the rest of the things should be separated out to focus on the trouble. Hence, trouble are minimize in their size because the person need not to be scared of everything in the world out there.

12 Rules for Life: Rule 11- Do Not Bother Children When They Are Skateboarding

People love to live their lives full of excitement. If one type of excitement ends, they move on to another type. Human nature wants the species to be able to do dangerous stunts but without harming self. Success may come along with the human tendency to first set itself straight. A human being evolves into a better person but also stays on the course of a passive-aggressive attitude towards self.

Chris, the author's friend mentioned earlier, died when he turned forty. He accomplished much by letting go of his limitations. He had to work through his resentment of others before he could reach the ultimate high.

The continuous judgment passed by people on things that matter, has resulted in a decline of the human state as the majority now considers the earlier judgment that was passed as the ultimate measure of all things, whether it is the subject of winning or losing, or being manly or being girly by indulging in something.

Modern society has changed the notions of what is required to live happily in the current circumstances. Males and females have an uneven playing field according to the author since the dominance has been handed over to the females and these females want to marry males that can handle them with their own dominating presence.

The author considers quite confidently that the culture actually empowers the females as the male is given the right to struggle towards fulfilling the needs of the females of the society. Humans have been pushed by the evolving cultures towards proving themselves as individuals while they should be looking for the good of the society as a whole.

While the attitude of the males is considered manly as long as it is inclined towards aggression, the author believes that they should start gaining female characteristics of being able to get along with people.

Boys should be raised like girls but boys do not actually learn their behavior from anywhere since they are born with these abilities. Someone just has to hone them or rather train them to let that side go.

12 Rules for Life: Rule 12- Pet a Cat When You Encounter One on the Street

Humans have a tendency to have favorites and all the favorites are similar to the individual themselves. Their own place in the world is right along with these people. The opposing unit is something that is disliked but it is due to the disliked group's presence that a person learns who to like at a given time. Groups that are joined by certain individuals are ones that help in their progression, but always the winning party would be chosen since no one wants to be amongst losers.

Humans have limitations. Of course they will have issues over brief periods of their lives but that does not mean that their life is not worth living. Life is precious regardless of one's limitations. Continuous craving for a limitless state where a human can have everything corrected in a blink of an eye would result in a crazed state of mind. Accept the situation and learn to live with it.

Humans have the capacity to overcome adversity as evidenced in the case of author's daughter Mikhaila. She went through various bone joint replacement surgeries and fought with her reliance on opioids. Additionally, this girl learned how to ride a bike for the sake of independence. Often, thinking of the negative side of life consumes the human mind. The author suggests that one should take out a fixed amount of time to think of the negativity of life and pass the rest of the time with a full purpose since life does not stop with the emergence of a new problem.

Cats, according to the author, are a lot like the higher being and once a cat shines upon a person, it brings a certain kind of refreshment to life. The author points out that while life may be as tough as it gets, you should take out some time to reflect upon and appreciate all the good things that life has given to the human race.

Background Information about the Summary of 12 Rules for Life: An Antidote to Chaos

12 Rules for Life: An Antidote to Chaos by Jordan B. Peterson was published in January 2018. The book responds to the need for guidance that arises with changing times. The book offers 12 fundamental rules to guide difference aspects of existence by finding a balance between old wisdom and convention and research in science. This is the kind of book that is for all ages and eras since it makes the subject of rules extremely simple and straightforward. It shares how to

lead life efficiently and restore order.

Background Information about the Author: Jordan B. Peterson

Jordan B. Peterson, who is from Canada, is a clinical psychologist, professor of psychology at the University of Toronto and a cultural critic. He has a B.A. degree in political science and a degree in psychology from the University of Alberta and a Ph.D. in clinical psychology from McGill University. He studies abnormal, social and personality psychology. Apart from *12 Rules for Life*, he has also written *Maps of Meaning: The Architecture of Belief*.

Discussion Questions about the Summary of 12 Rules for Life: An Antidote to Chaos

Do you agree with the rules presented in the book? Why or why not?

What is your favorite rule in the book and why?

Which rules do you apply in your life?

How important are the rules in life?

Do you want special deals?

Our mission is to bring you the highest quality companion books on the most popular books on the planet to enrichen and heighten your reading experience like never before!

We frequently give out free books or 0.99 discounted promotions on Amazon.

Be in the loop and receive special notifications by subscribing to our SpeedyReads membership mailing

list. By subscribing, you'll not only receive updates on the latest offer, you'll get "juicy" background information about novels you love, as well as a free copy of **"Delicious Reading: How to Quadruple and Enhance Your Book Reading Experience Within 24 Hours"** report and video package.

Check out:

http://www.easysummaries.com/gift

to sign up to SpeedyReads Free Membership!

FINAL SURPRISE BONUS

Hope you enjoyed this book as much as we enjoyed bring it to you!

I always like to overdeliver, so I'd like to give you one final bonus.

Do me a favor, if you enjoyed this book, please leave a review.   It'll help get the word out so more people can find out more about this wonderful book.

If you do, I'll send you a **FREE SECRET BONUS SECTIONS that didn't make it into this book! (including Trivia Games, Tantalizing Discussion Questions, etc!) (Worth $27)**

Here's what to do:

> 1. Leave a review (longer the better but we'd be grateful whichever length)
> 2. Send your review page URL as well as your username to: speedyreads24@gmail.com
> 3. Receive your bonus within a few hours after we check it!

That's it! Thanks again for purchasing this book and please be sure to check out our other high quality SpeedyReads books!

Warmly,

The SpeedyReadsTeam

CPSIA information can be obtained
at www.ICGtesting.com
Printed in the USA
LVOW11s0028040418
572241LV00001B/17/P